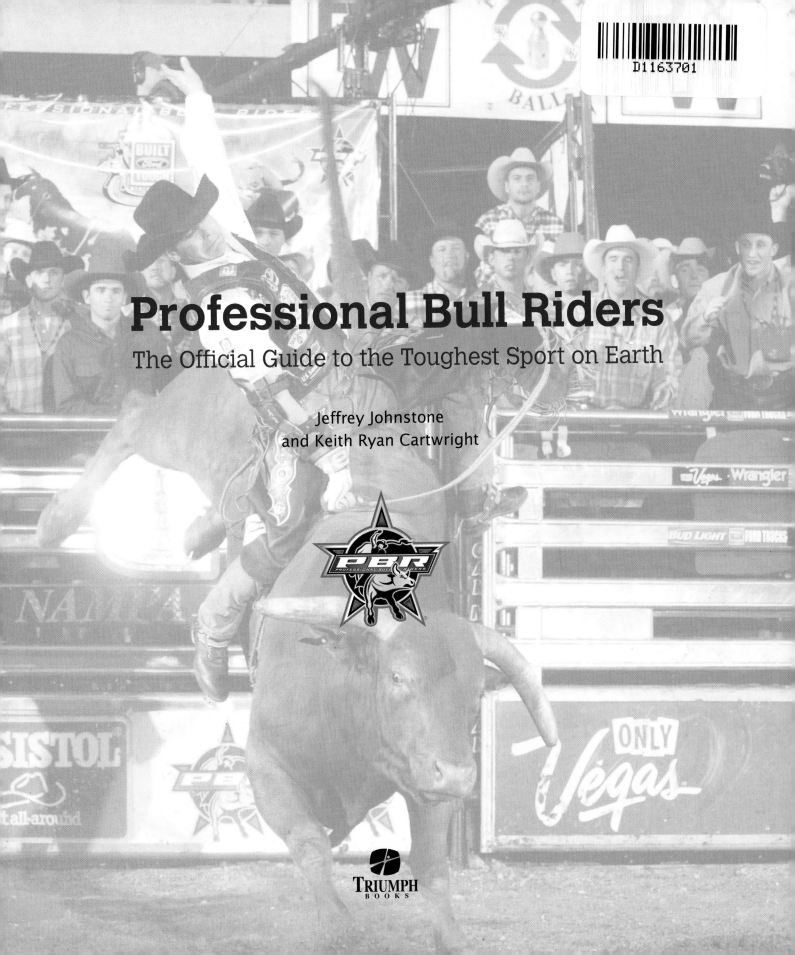

Professional Bull Riders

The Official Guide to the Toughest Sport on Earth

Jeffrey Johnstone
and Keith Ryan Cartwright

TRIUMPH
BOOKS

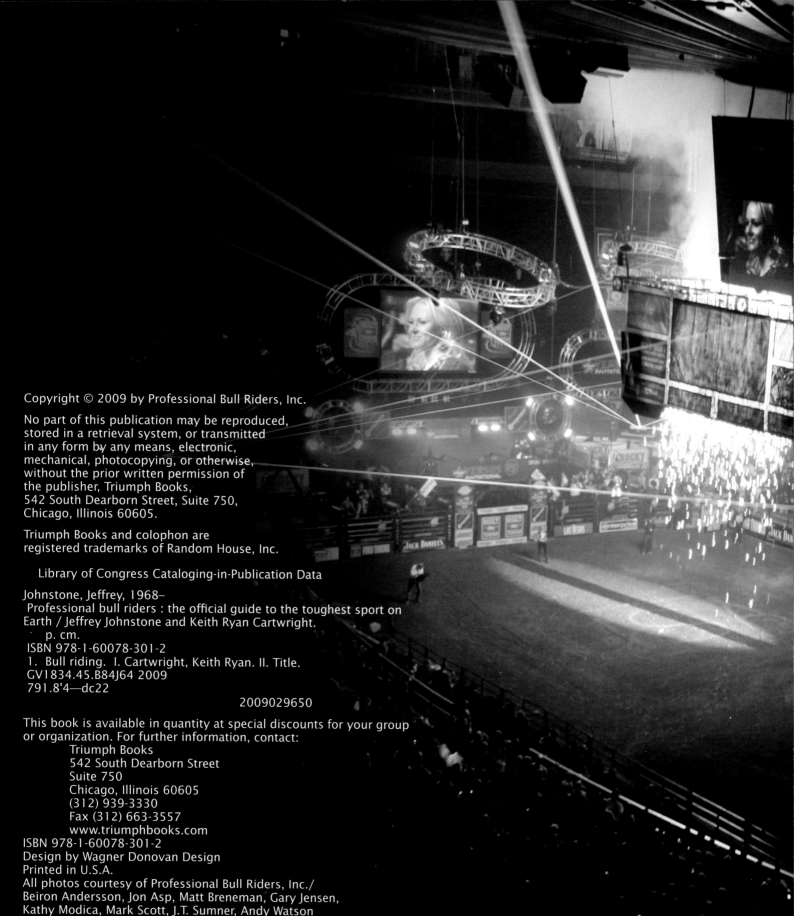

Library of Congress Cataloging-in-Publication Data

Johnstone, Jeffrey, 1968–
  Professional bull riders : the official guide to the toughest sport on
Earth / Jeffrey Johnstone and Keith Ryan Cartwright.
    p. cm.
  ISBN 978-1-60078-301-2
  1. Bull riding. I. Cartwright, Keith Ryan. II. Title.
  GV1834.45.B84J64 2009
  791.8'4—dc22
                              2009029650

This book is available in quantity at special discounts for your group
or organization. For further information, contact:
      Triumph Books
      542 South Dearborn Street
      Suite 750
      Chicago, Illinois 60605
      (312) 939-3330
      Fax (312) 663-3557
      www.triumphbooks.com
ISBN 978-1-60078-301-2
Design by Wagner Donovan Design
Printed in U.S.A.
All photos courtesy of Professional Bull Riders, Inc./
Beiron Andersson, Jon Asp, Matt Breneman, Gary Jensen,
Kathy Modica, Mark Scott, J.T. Sumner, Andy Watson

To Abigail and Hannah
—Jeff

For my mom, dad, and grandparents
—K.R.C.

Outweighed 10-to-1, bull riders rely on balance and a wiry strength unseen in most sports.

Contents

Ty Murray was in the Scottsdale, Arizona, hotel room the day the Professional Bull Riders was founded. His participation was a coup for the nascent organization; in his storied career, Murray claimed a record seven World All-Around Championships and two bull riding world titles. Past president of the PBR, his aggressive forays into mainstream popular culture have been critical in garnering attention for the sport. He currently lives in Stephenville, Texas, with his wife, singer-songwriter Jewel.

Introduction
Ty Murray

We have great fans in the PBR and from the Western way of life, and I was honored to have recently had a chance to represent everyone from our walk of life on Dancing with the Stars on ABC. The opportunity brought some great exposure and recognition to the cowboy and to the sport of bull riding.

When I first signed on to do the show, I realized that it wasn't going to be a cakewalk. In a lot of ways it reminded me of when we first had the idea to form the PBR, and all the work and unwavering try that we had to keep putting into it day after day in order to make it happen.

You have to go back to when it was 20 bull riders with an idea and understand how much we got laughed at, how many doors got shut in our face, and how we were told that the scenario was never going to work. When you think about it that way, it makes you realize that we must have believed very strongly in what we wanted to accomplish.

We shot for the stars from the very beginning.

A lot of the things we talked about back then, things that were a big joke to a lot of people, have become realities. We did have big dreams for the PBR, and we all decided that we were going to go at it with the bull rider's mentality: no matter what, just keep trying. When things got bad or things got tough, we wouldn't let that affect us—we would just keep reaching for what we believed.

Ty Murray continues to be a potent force in the sport he loves, serving as a broadcaster and as a board adviser to the PBR.

That's just what we did, and it's been a long, tough, rocky road to get to this point. And we definitely don't feel like we've arrived at any kind of destination. I think we work just as hard now and put just as much energy and thought into it as we ever have.

We've grown tremendously, but we will always have a lot of room to grow and improve as we try to show America—and the world, for that matter—what a great sport we have and what great athletes we have involved in our sport. We just have to keep working so that more people discover it, understand it, and follow it, so that they can appreciate it for how great we already know it is.

At times it's been unbelievable. You walk into a jam-packed arena and everyone there is excited and loving it. To think that I am a part of creating this is an amazing feeling.

It's not just an accident or luck that the PBR is thriving right now. It's taken a lot of work and a lot of adjustments to stay ahead of the game to keep things rolling during these tough economic times.

The one great thing that I have to come back to is that we have great fans. They are true blue, dyed-in-the-wool, hard-core fans who appreciate and support what we're doing and know what we stand for. That's the thing about the cowboy culture: there's a strong bond that holds all of us together.

—Ty Murray
PBR Cofounder

1997 World Champion Michael Gaffney and three-time World Champion Bull Little Yellow Jacket put on a show in Nampa in 2004, combining for 96.5 points and tying the record for the highest-marked ride in PBR history.

This Is Not a Rodeo

Chapter One

Listen.

In five minutes, this arena will open its doors to 15,000 strong. Amplified voices will soon pierce the air. Television lights will engulf the ring in their fire. The foundations will shake with the thunder of cheers and stomps.

But now, in the dark and the quiet, listen.

Listen for the ghosts. They are the shades of three centuries' worth of men who lived by their own rules. Men who poured their blood and sweat into the very dirt that now covers the arena floor. These are heroes who dared. These are cowboys.

Professional Bull Riders is the end result of their 300-year evolution. Tonight, the greatest athletes to ever wear spurs will carry on their tradition. They will risk everything they've known—their homes, families, indeed, their very lives—for one eight-second ride.

They will ride for the money. They will ride for the glory. And, perhaps most important, they will ride for the ghosts.

It began as a dream.

Twenty men, $20,000, and the kind of determination only a bull rider can understand. Almost two decades ago, a group of 20 bull riders had had enough. Sure, they loved rodeo and its trappings—the flaxen-haired beauties with their flags, the horses whose magnificence defies description, and the skill of the cowboys who explode out of a chute and wrap a rope around a speeding steer. They still love it.

But traditional rodeo—a combination of calf roping, team roping, barrel racing, saddle bronc, bareback, steer wrestling, and bull riding—had its limitations for bull riders. For one, getting a good bull was a crap shoot. In the early 1990s, there were so many rodeos in so many different places across country that the probability of getting a quality animal was slim. And in a sport where half the score is earned by the animal, that was a problem.

There was a reason why promoters always held bull riding until the end of the show. It is the same reason that the Romans packed the Coliseum: danger. Injuries are common in all Western sports—there's certainly nothing delicate about steer wrestling—but bull riding was different. Men can be—and are—killed every year. But when it came time to hit the pay window, the pot was out of whack. The men who brought the crowds left with no more than anyone else.

"We always knew bull riding was way more dangerous than any other event in rodeo," said Cody Lambert, a PBR founding father. "But we got paid exactly the same [amount]. We were carrying more than our share of the load, but we weren't being rewarded any more than anyone else."

Many of the men who regularly sacrificed their bodies for the sport had come away from the sport with nothing at all. World Champions were flat broke upon retirement.

Lambert had spent his career in the traditional rodeo system. He'd seen his own childhood heroes fade into obscurity with little more to show for it than a permanent limp and a stack of unpaid bills.

"We were looking at guys who had been champions or nearly champions—who were our heroes when we were

"Let's go, men!" A nod of the head and the crash of the gate, and the clock starts ticking—the toughest eight seconds in professional sports.

growing up—and they ended up with nothing at the end of it all. When their bull riding career was over, they didn't know how to do anything else," he said.

In 1992, 20 of the best bull riders in the world sat in a Scottsdale, Arizona, hotel room and came up with a plan. If they could form a united front and stick together, they could stop getting nickel-and-dimed by small-time rodeos. Their idea was to present the best riders in the world on the best bulls in the world, and maybe have something to show for it at the end of the day. They each put down $1,000.

Michael Gaffney, the future 1997 World Champion, was there that day. He recalls, "I think it was the weekend before I dislocated my riding shoulder for the first time, after I hit the ground real bad—that was in El Paso—and I ended up getting on that bull in the short go in Scottsdale and won. I think I received a check that day for $860-some. When I called home after writing that $1,000 check and told [my wife] Robin, she said, 'You wrote a check for what?' My entry fees were over $200 and we were dead, crack broke by the time I paid the IRS. We were in bad shape. And I had just won the NFR (National Finals Rodeo)!"

But he did it. They all did. Key sponsorships were lined up, and in 1994 a 27-year-old fair promoter named Randy Bernard became Chief Executive Officer of Professional Bull Riders, Inc. The rest, as they say, is history.

The inaugural 1994 season featured eight events and a total purse of just $250,000. Today, a season features over 30 events; the total purse is over $11 million.

When the PBR made its television debut in 1995, 12 million viewers tuned in. In 2008 17 million people watched world finals—17 million people in the People's Republic of China, that is.

When the majority share of PBR was sold to Spire Capital Partners in 2007, the $1,000 each rider had contributed in Scottsdale had grown to over $4 million.

In 2009, in the midst of a worldwide recession, attendance was down across the sporting world. Even professional football and baseball saw sales slump. Smaller sports went out of business completely. But at the PBR, attendance swelled by 12 percent.

In bull riding, it's not a matter of if you'll get hurt, it's when and how bad.

Kody Lostroh may be the most technically perfect rider in the world. He ought to be—he's been studying bull riding since the age of six, when he found (and subsequently wore out) a videotape of the Cheyenne Frontier Days Rodeo. The Colorado cowboy was named the PBR's Rookie of the Year in 2005, and has finished in the top 10 every season since.

The most coveted prize in Western sports, the PBR World Champion Gold Buckle costs over $10,000 and comes with a $1 million bonus, but its real value is immeasurable.

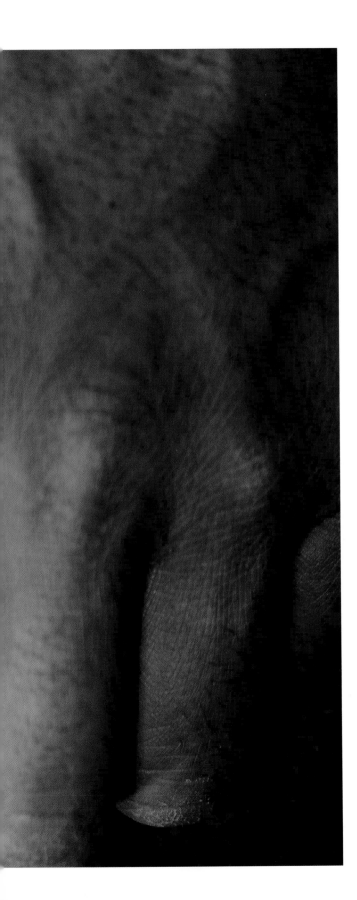

In less than two decades, the Professional Bull Riders have turned what used to be a county fair spectacle into a sparkling, massive, worldwide phenomenon.

A century from now, the world will surely be a different place. The great Western expanse that chiseled the cowboy from its own rocky heart may well be gone. Heroes may be in short supply.

But in an arena not yet built, a young man we will never meet will stand and tip his hat to a crowd that has yet to be born. And on that day, some small part of all that is strong, and brave, and good will live on. All thanks to 20 men and a dream. ✪

"Try" is a noun in cowboy parlance. It's determination, effort, and persistence. And it's often the only thing between a qualified ride and a face full of dirt.

Bull Riding: A Primer

With one hand, hang on to the bull for eight seconds.

Of course, that's like saying basketball is putting a ball through a hoop, or ballet is just foot movement.

In bull riding, careers are built or destroyed, reputations made or lost, and lives fulfilled or snuffed out in an eight-second span. From the moment the gate opens, every muscle in the body is engaged. It's about strength and balance, move and countermove.

The rules, however, are simple.

The clock starts when the bull's shoulder or hip breaks the plane of the gate. It stops when the rider's hand comes out of the rope.

Four judges rate each rider and each bull on a scale from one to 25. Those points are added together and divided in half to reach a score between zero and 50 for both the rider and the bull. Those final numbers are then added together to reach a final ride score between zero and 100.

A cowboy is judged on how well he matches the bull's moves and maintains control of the ride. He cannot touch anything with his free arm. Extra points are awarded for style; spurring, for example, demonstrates control.

A bull is judged on his athleticism, which takes into account spin (right or left), direction changes (contrasted with spin, a switch in movement forward or backward or side to side), kick in the back end, drop in the front, height of jumps, and overall difficulty to ride.

Any score over 90 points is considered a great ride—a "home run" of bull riding. The highest score ever earned in the PBR was a 96.5, a feat accomplished by three different riders: Chris Shivers, Michael Gaffney, and Bubba Dunn. ✪

Every cowboy has his own way of preparing for a ride. Some stretch, some hop around, and some listen to music. Some others pray. Here, 18-year-old Ryan Dirteater wraps rawhide around his wrist to keep his glove from being torn off during the ride. Dirteater, a full-blooded Cherokee from Hubert, Oklahoma, is representative of many of the young riders on the PBR. The confidence and swagger of a bull rider is present, but so is a notable humility and courtesy. It's always "Yes, sir" and "No, ma'am," "Please" and "Thank you." Newcomers to the sport are often surprised by politeness and accessibility of PBR athletes.

❶ Bull Rope

The bull rope is custom-made, with a loop about three to five feet around on one end. A leather handle is woven into the body of the rope. The handle is placed against the center of the bull's back; the loose end of the rope (tail) is wrapped around the chest of the bull, directly behind the animal's front legs. The tail is then threaded through the loop at the other end, then doubled back into the rider's hand.

A metal bell hangs from the bottom of the rope, giving it enough weight so that the entire apparatus slips off easily once the rider lets go.

❷ Flank Strap

The flank strap is just that: a strap, often lined with sheepskin, placed around the flank of the bull. Its purpose is to enhance the natural bucking motion of the animal by giving him something to try to kick off.

The flank strap never goes around the bull's genitals and no sharp objects are ever placed inside the flank strap to agitate the animal. Not surprisingly, like humans, bulls aren't likely to jump, run, and kick if their genitals are bound. The strap is designed for quick release and is removed immediately after the bull exits the arena.

❸ Spurs

Spurs help the rider maintain his balance by giving him added grip with his feet. Bull riding spurs have dull rowels (wheels) that are loosely locked into place. Unlike horses, bulls have loose skin that has a degree of "roll" to it. The bull's hide, which is seven times thicker than human skin, is not cut by the rider's spurs.

❹ Chaps

Leather chaps protect the cowboy's legs from both the bull and the steel chutes. Custom-made and worth up to several thousand dollars, each rider has chaps with his own unique colors, designs, and sponsor logos on them. The fringe on the sides, a traditional decorative accent, helps bring the judges' attention to the rider's legwork.

❺ Glove

A single glove protects the riding hand from the intense pressure and friction of the bull rope during the ride. Riders usually tape or tie the glove around the wrist to prevent it from slipping off during the ride.

❻ Vest

Invented by PBR Stock Director Cody Lambert, the protective vest the cowboy wears absorbs shock and dissipates blows to the body, helping prevent internal injuries. Made of leather and thick foam, the vest is surprisingly lightweight and is built to tear away in the event of a hooking.

❼ Cowboy Hat/Helmet

The PBR leaves the choice of headwear up to the individual rider. Many choose to wear only a cowboy hat out of a sense of tradition, or because they feel helmets interfere with balance and vision. Often, cowboys will wear a helmet and/or mask after a particularly nasty face or head injury. The helmet is similar to that worn in hockey, with some adaptations. For example, the lower bar of the face mask is removed to allow the rider to tuck his chin against his chest.

In a tangle of braids and leather, a bull rider can spot his rope like his own child in a crowd. The rope is as individual as he is; each is custom-made to his personal specifications. They come in plaits (rhymes with "flats") or braids, with a five-plait being the softest and loosest, and a nine-plait stiff and tight. Most Brazilian riders use the stiffer nine-plait, since a shortage of poly-blend materials in Brazil requires that organic rope be woven particularly strong.

No matter the size of the crowd, bull riding still comes down to eight desperate seconds of man versus beast. It's part balancing act, part strength, and all adrenaline.

The athletes of the PBR demonstrate a camaraderie unseen in other sports. Hard-core competitors will laugh, train, and even travel together. Perhaps it's the danger involved, but even the fiercest rivals will pull a rope, lend a piece of gear, and cheer each other on.

Wiley Petersen may be one of the best bull riders never to win a championship—yet. He is a perennial top-10 athlete, but has been held back by untimely injuries. Raised on the Shoshone-Bannock tribe's land in Fort Hall, Idaho, he is a man of deep faith and a joker behind the chutes.

Arguably the best bull rider of all time, Adriano Moraes won three World Championships, including the first-ever PBR title in 1994. A stickler for form and detail, his body awareness was unrivaled. Note the signature Moraes free hand: fingers held tight together, hand straight. Every move was calculated and practiced.

Harve Stewart has the enviable distinction of having grown up in Ty Murray's hometown of Stephenville, Texas, where Murray helped out the youngster early on.

One of the smallest bull riders on the Built Ford Tough Series circuit, New Mexico's Travis Briscoe is nonetheless one of the most talented. The 5'6" redhead has only been riding for four years, but has earned well over half a million dollars. In his first year on tour, Briscoe drew the legendary Little Yellow Jacket and topped him for 92 points.

"Down in the well." When the force of a bull's spin pulls the rider into the vortex, many things can happen, few of them good. Many bulls will actually try to avoid stepping on a downed rider, as their instinct is to protect their hooves and legs. They generally prefer to butt or hook.

Paulo Crimber demonstrates a slightly more desirable dismount: to the side and as far out from the bull as possible. Even though the dirt on the arena floor is about eight inches deep and the top four inches are kept fairly loose, there's simply no such thing as a soft landing.

Half of the score is up to the bull. Drop in the front end and kick in the back are important, as is the animal's ability to spin. A direction change, as contrasted with a change in rotation, is a change in the bull's overall motion backward, forward, or side to side.

Dirt explodes around Australian Brendon Clark at the 2008 World Finals. Australians have been a big part of the PBR from the beginning. 1998 World Champion Troy Dunn hails from there, and currently oversees the Australian branch of the PBR.

God and country play integral roles in the lives of PBR athletes and fans. Every show features patriotic pageantry.

2004 World Champion Mike Lee (above) prays before, during and after every event...not surprising, given the dangers involved in his chosen profession.

Once eight seconds have elapsed, the battle isn't over. Releasing yourself from the rope is vital. Part of Guilherme Marchi's success has been his uncanny ability to avoid injury, and that in turn is largely due to his picture-perfect form in both riding and dismounting a bull.

Kody Lostroh didn't ride with his left hand down until he was nine. When he made the switch, it clicked instantly.

The Thomas & Mack Center in Las Vegas—home of the PBR World Finals. For eight rounds in the fall, the storied venue is packed to the rafters with over 16,000 fans nightly.

Pain is part of the bull riding game. Before the implementation of Cody Lambert's padded vest, incidents like this were often fatal.

The most heralded of the recent crop of North Carolina riders, J.B. Mauney's loose riding style has taken him within spitting distance of the world title for three consecutive years. He will be the first PBR World Champion from east of the Mississippi if he succeeds.

There's no room for rivalry when it's time to ride. If an athlete needs a hand, any one of the other 39 top riders in the world

Style is a lesser consideration for Brazilian Renato Nunes. Leaning back, leaning forward, or even falling off the side, Nunes is famous for never giving up. His sheer heart and determination have earned him not only the respect and affection of his fellow riders, but numerous event wins and top-10 finishes.

"Don't tell your mother I showed you this." Bull riding is a family tradition for most of its participants. For over 140 years, cowboys have passed along the lifestyle to sons and grandsons.

The Cowboys

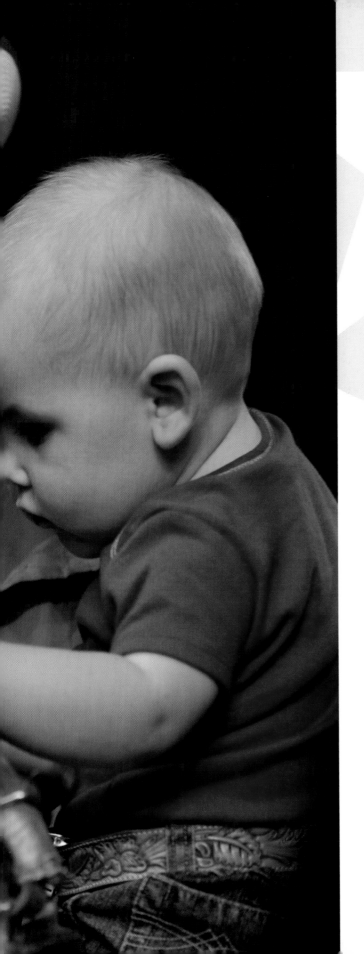

Chapter Two

What makes a cowboy? Traditionally, punching cattle and living on horseback. That might be less important today, but the cowboy archetype survives in its spirit and core values.

"The world has changed more than the cowboy, in my opinion, because they're the guys who get the job done and, no matter what the task, they do what it takes to get it done," said Cody Lambert, co-founder of the PBR and a 1996 inductee into its Ring of Honor.

A cowboy is someone who never gives up and is honest, both in his efforts and as a person.

Whether you're speaking of the 1800s, 1900s, or even the 21st century, the single-most important trait of a cowboy is the code of honor by which they live, which includes respect of women, children, and their elders; fidelity to those around them; straightforwardness; and, above all, honesty. A real cowboy must also be brave enough to step up and do the right thing.

Much of that tradition is rooted in sheer economics. In the old days, if a cattle boss was kind enough to hire a man on, he was obliged to demonstrate his loyalty. For years, and even in working-ranch rodeos today, a cowboy "rides for the brand" of his particular outfit.

Today, the tradition lives on, but loyalty has expanded to a cowboy's region. Riders are proud of where they come from. They work hard to uphold the reputation of their native soil. And that includes more than just performing well in the arena. It's about character. ✪

Two veterans walk the hallway of the Thomas & Mack Center in 2007, in what would be the last World Finals for both. J.W. Hart (left), known as "the Ironman" for originally setting the record for consecutive top-tour appearances, at a staggering 197, went on to work in the broadcast booth. Tater Porter (right), a former World Finals winner, has twice traveled to Afghanistan to entertain and visit with U.S. troops.

Pulling another rider's rope is often just a function of being in proximity when needed. While some riders prefer to have specific friends assist them, most are simply grateful for the help.

J.B. Mauney grew up under the tutelage of the great Jerome Davis, the 1995 PRCA World Champion. Davis' presence in North Carolina has helped the Tar Heel State become a new locus of bull riding talent.

Breaking from Tradition

The image of the American cowboy has long been associated with the Western way of life.

Historically, most bull riders have hailed from states like Texas, Oklahoma, Colorado, Wyoming, New Mexico, and Arizona. No one bull rider typified the bull riding tradition more than Jim Shoulders, the Oklahoman widely known as "the Babe Ruth of Rodeo." But some riders flocked to bull riding from far-flung destinations. Larry Mahan was from Oregon and represented the Pacific Northwest. The original urban cowboy was Bobby Del Vecchio, who hailed from the East Coast—the Bronx, to be exact. Myron Duarte traveled across the Pacific from Hawaii to compete.

In recent years, as the PBR has continued to grow in popularity and visibility, the sport of bull riding has transcended regional boundaries. The world standings reads like a geography lesson. Just as riding percentages and monies earned continue to rise, the list of riders' hometowns is ever-expanding. It stretches from North Carolina to Florida all the way west to Oregon, with check marks on a map representing card-carrying members of the PBR from every geographical region in the continental United States. Today, membership in the PBR totals over 1,200.

Like Mahan decades before him, Ross Coleman comes from Oregon, where he also hosts an annual Challenger event each summer in his hometown of Molalla. In fact, the Ross Coleman Invitational was twice voted by the fellow riders as the PBR Minor League Event of the Year.

So it shouldn't come as a surprise that the area surrounding the Oregon Trail would be rich with talent. In recent years, two up-and-coming young guns, Cody Ford and Cody Campbell, have emerged from Oregon. Ford, 20, established himself one of the future faces of the PBR when he won his first-ever Built Ford Tough Series event in 2009. He took home more than $60,000 at a one-day event in Glendale, Arizona. His friend Campbell, 21, has also gone to great lengths to prove himself as a gutty Coleman-like cowboy.

But no part of the country has proved a more fertile breeding ground than North Carolina. Jerome Davis, a 1995 PRCA (Pro Rodeo Cowboys Association) World Champion and 1998 inductee to the Ring of Honor, was one of the first great bull riders to call attention to Tobacco Road. As a mentor to a new generation of athletes, North Carolina has become a destination for dozens of would-be hopefuls.

Shane Proctor recently relocated to the Tar Heel State to train with Brian Canter, as well as his brother-in-law, J.B. Mauney. Canter, who elicits comparisons to the legendary Lane Frost, and Mauney provide the organization with its best opportunity in years of boasting a world champion from east of the Mississippi River.

These days, for every Mike Lee and Mike White (Texas) or Ryan Dirteater and Austin Meier (Oklahoma), there's Chris Shivers and Nick Landreneau (Louisiana), Luke Snyder and Matt Bohon (Missouri), or Sean Willingham and Kasey Hayes (Georgia).

The age of mass media has smashed borders and frontiers, and the PBR has gone along for the ride. These days, a map is little more than a way to find the next event. ✪

The current depth of talent in the PBR is greater than any time in history. There have always been a few hypertalented standouts in bull riding, but today the talent gap between the top and bottom is narrower than ever.

Countermoves are crucial, particularly when a rider finds himself rocketing toward a 18-inch-wide head festooned with what amounts to a baseball bat on each side. The constant effort to remain centered gives bull riders the strongest core muscles in professional sports.

A belly roll—a full-body twist with all four hooves in the air—can test even the most talented riders. Those who manage to hang on will find their scores soaring.

Though it will wear through over the course of a season, a cowboy takes great care of his bull rope. It is his lifeline.

McKennon Wimberley has a leg up on most other riders—the Texas youngster is also a Golden Gloves boxer. Stretching like this is difficult for even seasoned athletes. Doing it in Wranglers is pretty much impossible.

Sometimes it takes a little self-abuse to get fired up. Guilherme Marchi prepares to descend onto a bovine opponent in Madison Square Garden. The few seconds spent seated on a bull in the chute are the rider's most vulnerable.

Up close, the size difference between man and bull becomes alarmingly clear. Bulls generally run in the 1,500-pound range, though some can top out at over a ton.

Rosin darkens the well-worn gloves and ropes of the PBR elite, a sticky testament to past battles. By the end of the night, any of these pieces of equipment could be torn to pieces.

The exact reason for the ascendancy of Brazilian athletes in the PBR is subject to debate. Perhaps it is because there are simply more bull riders in Brazil, where the nation's cattle herd outnumbers that of the U.S. by two to one. Perhaps it's because those riders good enough to get to the States are already world-class athletes by the time they reach the Built Ford Tough Series. Perhaps they are less given to the hell-raising lifestyle of many American cowboys. Whatever the reason, they've raised the bar of competition to new heights. Pictured, from left to right: Renato Nunes, Helton Barbosa, Robson Palermo, and Valdiron de Oliveira.

The Killer Bs

In late 1993, Adriano Moraes returned to the U.S. for what was then his second trip. Already a champion in Brazil, Moraes was considered one of the best bull riders in the world. Naturally, the co-founders of the PBR invited the young Brazilian to compete with them.

"The Brazilian Guy" eventually won the first gold buckle awarded by the PBR. But his success translated into much more. Moraes practically single-handedly gave what had been considered an American sport the face of a handsome foreigner. Bull riding was no longer a stand-alone spectacle. It had become an international phenomenon.

He was not the first foreign rider to compete in the circuit. But in winning the 1994 world title and garnering a growing number of sponsors along the way, he was inarguably the first successful one. There was something different, something special, about the Brazilian guy with the wide smile.

In the years since, one Brazilian after another has followed in Moraes' footsteps. From Paulo Crimber to Ednei Caminhas to, more recently, riders such as Robson Palermo and Valdiron de Oliveira, an ever-growing number of countrymen have all been afforded the opportunity to escape poverty because of what Moraes accomplished all those years ago.

By coming to compete in the PBR, the Brazilian riders have not only achieved success in the arena, but they have created better lives, including better homes for their families and better education for their children.

"What I did wasn't any more than just being at the right place at the right time at the right moment in history," Moraes explained. "It's not just the right time, it's the right moment in history.

"So I believe that Adriano Moraes changed the faith and face of bull riding [and] the profession in Brazil, but still it just happened to be me." ✪

Stories and jokes are shared in the locker room, just as they are with American athletes, except in Portuguese. For many Brazilians, it's vital to stay on the Built Ford Tough Series, as the language barrier can be insurmountable at lower-level events.

Tears stream down the face of Adriano Moraes after the final ride of his career at the World Finals in 2008. Few, if any, bull riders have had the impact Moraes has had on the evolution of the sport.

Adriano Moraes, the godfather of Brazilian athletes. The eventual three-time World Champion came to America on the advice of 1982 PRCA champion bull rider Charlie Sampson. Rumor has it that when a U.S. reporter wanted a translator for a live interview early in Moraes' career, Sampson volunteered, though he didn't speak a word of Portuguese. As the cameras rolled, the reporter asked "Why did you start riding bulls?" Without batting an eye, Sampson chimed in, slowly and loudly: "WYEE DEED YOU START RIDEEING BOOLS?"

Renato Nunes launches himself off the rails to celebrate another successful ride. The sheer enthusiasm of the Brazilian athletes has won the hearts of PBR fans worldwide.

A blur of red, black, and yellow tears onto the Las Vegas dirt as Robson Palermo conquers yet another bull on his way to the 2008 World Finals event title. Palermo grew up without electricity in a town in the Amazon rainforest so remote it takes seven hours to get there from Sao Paulo—by plane. For seven days of effort in Vegas, he collected over $321,000.

Charismatic and enormously talented, the perpetually smiling Guilherme Marchi has become the single-most consistent rider in PBR history, with a career riding percentage of over 63 percent. From 2005 to 2007, he spent three frustrating seasons at number two in the world.

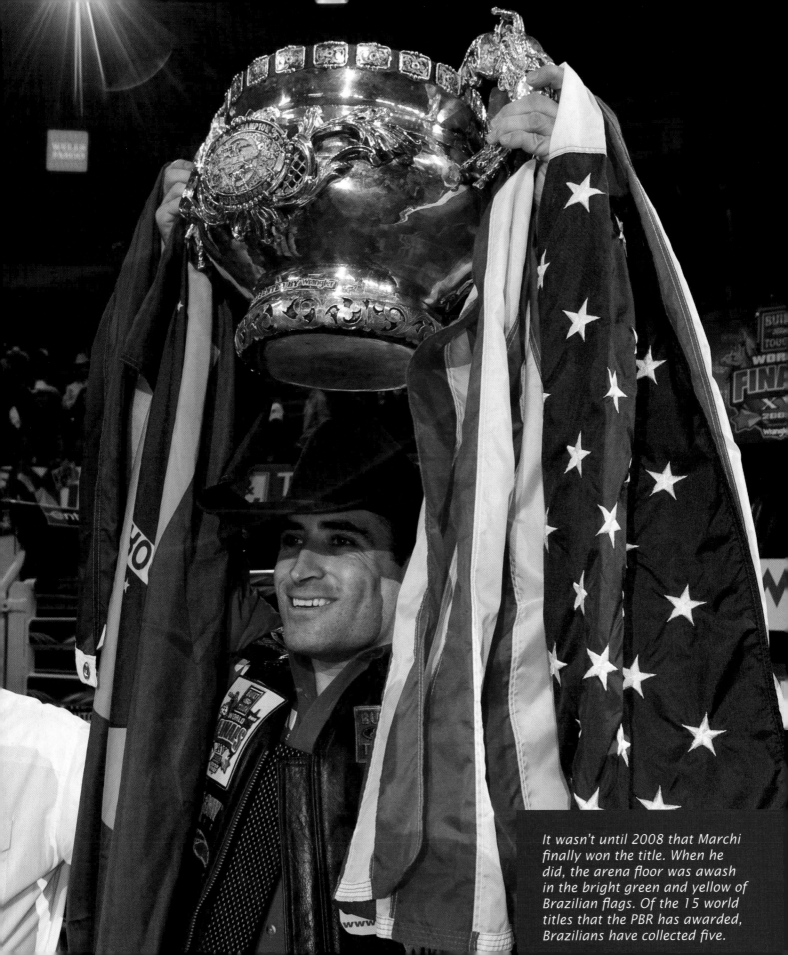

It wasn't until 2008 that Marchi finally won the title. When he did, the arena floor was awash in the bright green and yellow of Brazilian flags. Of the 15 world titles that the PBR has awarded, Brazilians have collected five.

Guilherme Marchi is renowned for his astounding pound-for-pound strength. His workout, featured in Men's Fitness magazine, involves standing in a pool and using the water's resistance to build core muscles.

Marchi is one of those men whose presence lights up a room—or an arena, as the case may be. Perhaps the greatest active bull rider in the world, he is also one of the most accessible, never refusing an autograph or photo request.

A deeply religious man, Marchi practices his Catholic faith with a quiet fervor. "You have exalted my strength," reads Psalm 92, "like that of a wild ox."

The Brazil–U.S. bull rider pipeline has opened opportunities for scores of young athletes, including Leonil Santos. Santos dominated the Brazilian tour in 2008, and late in the year not only found himself at the World Finals, but in the running for Rookie of the Year.

Two world champions, Ednei Camhinas (right) and Adriano Moraes (middle), yuk it up with relative newcomer Valdiron de Oliveria, who in two short years on tour has established himself as a title contender. "Oh, he is going to be a world champion," said Moraes of the newcomer. "There's no doubt. He has the mind for it, so it's only a matter of time."

Mud, blood, and glory are all a part of the game, as a slightly dazed Chris Shivers shows following a ride at the 2008 World Finals. Shivers endured two massive facial injuries that year, leading the old-school cowboy to exchange his familiar white hat for a hard plastic helmet.

One of the toughest cowboys on tour, Ross Coleman's decision to switch to a helmet coincided with the birth of his son. The Madison Square Garden event in January 2009 marked the first time in PBR history that more riders wore helmets than hats.

Perhaps the greatest bull to ever kick dirt, Little Yellow Jacket won an unprecedented three World Champion Bull titles in his career. The bent-horned brangus loved the sport, often strutting around the arena after bucking off his latest victim. He's currently enjoying a well-earned retirement in North Carolina.

The Bulls

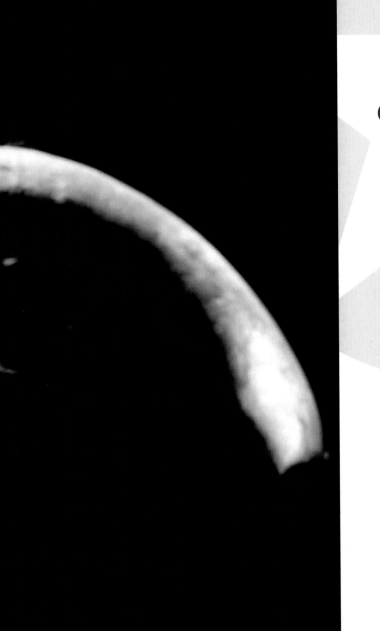

Chapter Three

The PBR is about being the best. And in bull riding, the bull is just as important as its rider.

"It was easy for us to know we had the best bull riders in the world," said Cody Lambert, PBR livestock director. "We needed worthy opponents for them, so we made every effort to make sure we had the best bulls that were available." It was that kind of competition that would broaden the interest of the sport.

Imagine, if you will, the Chicago Bulls traveling playing an exhibition game against a local high school team. It wouldn't have nearly the same impact as an NBA Finals matchup with the Los Angeles Lakers. The same concept holds true with the PBR. The organization prides itself on matching the very best athletes against the very best opponents.

And so, in the PBR, bulls are considered to be animal athletes.

"Champions have qualities that won't allow them to lose," Lambert stated. "They have a work ethic that won't allow them to fail. The best bulls of the 1950s, '60s, '70s, '80s, and '90s—the very best are just like the champions of today."

The rankest bulls in the pen don't jump higher or kick harder or spin any faster than they did 20 or 30 years ago. The difference is simply that there are a lot more good ones.

People and bulls have physical gifts and physical abilities, but it is a rare combination of skill and commitment to excellence that elevates an athlete to become a champion. That athlete is willing to pay the price by working harder than the rest.

In the PBR, three bulls have stood taller than all the others: Little Yellow Jacket, Dillinger, and Mossy Oak Mudslinger. All three were very different animals with distinctly unique personalities. But they had one thing in common: they were all dedicated athletes and competitors.

Though other bull riding organizations have occasionally played up particular bulls, no one's done it quite like the PBR. Keeping the emphasis on "two great athletes in every ride," the PBR has created bovine superstars. Even today, fans of Little Yellow Jacket will travel cross-country for a glimpse of the great bull.

Little Yellow Jacket

"No bull or bull rider loved the sport more than Little Yellow Jacket," said Lambert, had seen him once in competition in 1999 and later that year took him to his first PBR World Finals, where Ty Murray said, "That's one little bucking son of a gun."

Little Yellow Jacket would go on to be the only bull to have been named PBR World Champion Bull three consecutive years (2002–04). It's no wonder he's considered by many to be the most distinguished bull in PBR history. Known for his explosiveness leaving the chutes, he was revered not only for his athleticism—speed, kick, and ability to change directions—but also for his intelligence. It's been said he knew enough to relax, drink water, and take care of himself.

There were times he would kick so high and be turning back at the same time that he might stumble just a little bit with his front legs, but he would never hesitate or even slow down to get his feet back under him. Instead, he would buck right through any glitch in his rhythm and continue to put out even more effort.

"He was always in the short go," Lambert said, "which means not only was he at the Built Ford Tough Series against the best bull riders in the world, but he was against the Top 15 bull riders that week...and he always came through."

He didn't just enjoy competing, he wanted to compete. If he was grazing in a 1,000-acre pasture and you pulled a trailer in and opened the gate, Little Yellow Jacket would come running and jump right in it on his own. It didn't matter how far he had traveled to an event, what the weather was like, or how bright the lights were—he always came to the arena to put on a show.

In a seven-year career he never once failed, and according to Lambert, "He knew his job was to buck that rider off." The dark red Brangus bull with his easily identifiable downward-curving left horn was involved in two of the most historic rides in PBR history. The first was in 2003 when Chris Shivers challenged Little Yellow Jacket in the

Bud Light Million-Dollar Bounty presented by Ford Trucks. The bull, who has six of the top 50 scored rides of all time, rose to the occasion and had one of the best trips of his career, which is saying a lot for a bull who was only ridden 14 times in 90 attempts and threw riders to the dirt in an average of 2½ seconds. As usual, he leapt high out of the chutes and dropped his front end to the ground, throwing Shivers forward and off balance. In less than two seconds, it was over. As the two-time World Champion hit the dirt, Little Yellow Jacket, as he always did, paraded in a small circle with his head held high before walking through the out gate. He didn't take more than a few seconds to leave, but he owned it.

A year later, at a 2004 event in Nampa, Idaho, was matchup featuring two great world champions in the twilight of their careers. Michael Gaffney pulled a tight rope and held on past that trademark first drop. Little Yellow Jacket tended to lead with left foot, but occasionally he would spin to the right. On this day, for some reason, he went to the right, but Gaffney countered perfectly and with his adjustment he made the whistle. According to Lambert, G-Man "made a great ride and everything just fit together" to the tune of a record-tying score for the highest marked ride in PBR history: 96.5 points.

Six months later, the two met up again in the eighth round of the PBR World Finals. It would be the last ride of Gaffney's illustrious career and the New Mexican cowboy stuck it on him for 93.75 points.

"How could you end a World Championship career better than on the biggest stage in the most important round. And Little Yellow Jacket came through like he always did," said Lambert.

Four years into his retirement, Little Yellow Jacket lives on a ranch in North Carolina where his owner, Tom Teague, swells at the mention of his star stud. There's not a bull alive who meant as much to the PBR as Little Yellow Jacket and perhaps his sons will carry on that legacy.

"Little Yellow Jacket loved competing so much that he saved every ounce of energy for the arena," Lambert said. "He was the ultimate PBR athlete."

Michael Gaffney and Little Yellow Jacket were an eye-popping team. In addition to a 93.75-point score at the 2004 World Finals, the pair posted an astounding 96.5 points at Nampa in 2004, tying the all-time PBR record. Gaffney's final ride on Little Yellow Jacket was one of the things that convinced him to retire. "That ride put the perfect period on my career," he said.

Cody Lambert

No one knows bulls better than Cody Lambert. In fact, no single bull rider has had a bigger impact on the PBR. Aside from his distinguished riding career, he played a significant role as co-founder of the PBR, a member of the Board of Directors, a former judge, and the architect of the protective vest worn by all bull riders.

He also single-handedly developed the role of PBR livestock director. Under his guidance, stock contractors have become as important to the sport as the riders themselves, and breeding has become a multi-million dollar industry that has revolutionized professional bull riding.

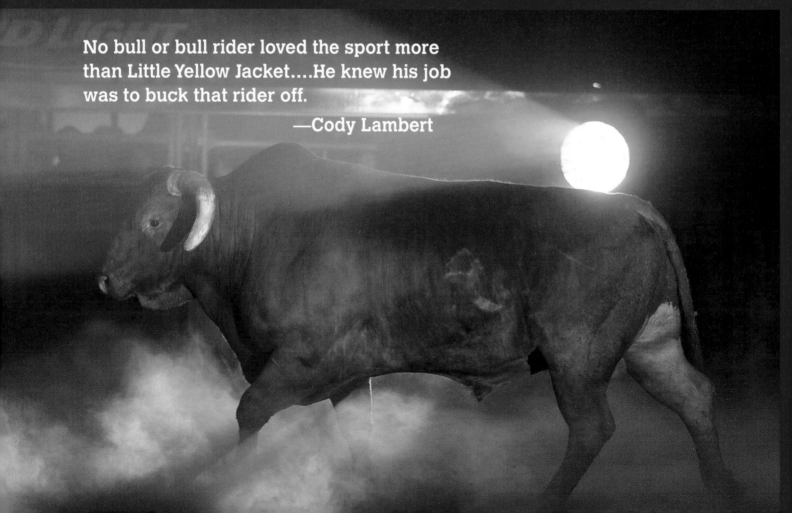

No bull or bull rider loved the sport more than Little Yellow Jacket....He knew his job was to buck that rider off.

—Cody Lambert

Little Yellow Jacket loved the spotlight. Head held high, the usually victorious bull would sometimes need a little prompting from the safety rider to head back to the pens and the well-deserved feed trough. Five of the 50 highest-scoring rides of all time involved Little Yellow Jacket.

One-horned and surly, Dillinger won consecutive World Champion Bull titles in 2000 and 2001.

Dillinger

Weighing in at over 1,800 pounds, Dillinger was a big bull, but, more importantly, he was an athletic one. An incredibly muscular animal, Dillinger could jump higher and spin faster than any other bull, despite his size.

"He was a freak because of his athletic ability," said Lambert, who likened the bull to fearsome NFL linebacker Lawrence Taylor. The two had size, speed, and determination that set them apart from the crowd.

"Because of his size and strength, he was the one bull that struck fear in most guys who got on him," Lambert continued. "It took a champion to ride him, and the champions had to have a great day."

Dillinger naturally had the speed and agility of bulls that weighed far less and he had the strength and power of any bull his size. At first, Dillinger was not considered to be a natural competitor in the same way that some of the other all-time great bulls were. It wasn't until he was five years old that he really came into his own as a revered bucking bull.

Early on, he was known for being more than a little wild in the chute. One infamous story involving a young and unruly Dillinger took place in January 1999 at a rodeo in Ft. Worth, Texas, when he jumped over the back of a chute and actually got into the building on the concourse level.

"He was running up and down there and ran over some people," Lambert recalled. "He caused quite a wreck...and ran over people who were at the popcorn stand."

Later that year, in August, he went to a Challenger event in Weatherford, Texas, where he wasn't even considered the best bull in the pen. But just two and a half months later, at the 1999 PBR World Finals, he was without question the best.

In 2000, he won the first of his back-to-back World Championships. Widely feared, Dillinger bucked off nearly 86 percent of his riders and sports one of the most impressive career bull score averages, 46.16 points. Few cowboys wanted to match up with Dillinger, and even fewer can boast what it was like to make the eight-second whistle. One of the few was Jim Sharp. The legendary rider won nearly $85,000 for the accomplishment. For the few who made the whistle, Dillinger provided four of the top 50 scores of all time.

Dillinger was on his way to his third world title when he broke his leg, a tragic incident in which the veteran bucker actually broke his leg before he came out of the chute.

"He still bucked harder for eight seconds on three legs than most bulls can on four," Lambert said.

Due in large part to his freakish nature, Dillinger is considered by many to be the best bull to have ever bucked in the PBR.

Blueberry Wine represented one of the two extremes of PBR bulls. He was much smaller than most, but could spin like category-5 tornado. Overshadowed by Little Yellow Jacket during most of his career, he was still a top contender for the world title in most of his competition years.

The bulls of the PBR are bred to buck. There is an anticipation in their eyes while they await their turn in the chutes. Veterans will keep still until the gate opens, while younger bulls will often lunge or rear back, creating enormous danger for the rider in the coffin-shaped metal cage.

Mossy Oak Mudslinger, another fan favorite, won his world title in 2006, in the twilight of his career. The mid-sized bull was revered for his consistency and try. In four years on tour at the highest level of competition, Mudslinger had exactly two off days—and even so, his rides scored in the high 80s.

Mossy Oak Mudslinger

"He was a bull that absolutely had all the tools," Lambert says.

Mossy Oak Mudslinger looked great. He may have been an average-sized bull—he bucked his entire career at anywhere from 1,400 to 1,500 pounds—but he had big horns. He was athletic and physical, but, more importantly, he was a true competitor.

"From 100 yards away," Lambert said, "you could see that he was an athlete just by the way he carried himself."

Mudslinger came of age in the PBR. The first time he bucked in the PBR World Finals, he was just three years old. Ridden just 27 times in 93 career BFTS outs, only four times was he scored under 90 points, and even then, he was never scored below 88 points.

One of his greatest outs came in 2001 when Adam Carrillo scored 94.5 points at an event in Columbus, Georgia.

"When you think of the best rides ever, there are so many in the PBR that some get overlooked," Lambert said, "and that's one of them."

Throughout his entire career, Mudslinger had just two off days—and even then riders still scored in the high-80s. When he was all of two years old, Mudslinger's owner H.D. Page bucked him for the first time with a mechanical dummy on his back. Unfortunately, the remote malfunctioned and they were unable to release the dummy. He was young and mean, so the stock contractor and several others couldn't get close enough to release the dummy by hand. As frustration set in, Mudslinger kept trying to buck it off, and when he finally tired, he fell to the ground only to get right back up and keep going. It would have ruined most other young bulls, but not Mudslinger.

"He would not give up," Lambert said. "He had it. He had no quit in him." Thought of as a perfect gentleman in the chute, the only reason Mossy Oak Mudslinger wasn't a multi-year World Champion Bull was because throughout his stellar career he finished his first four years behind either Dillinger or Little Yellow Jacket before finally becoming a World Champion as he neared the end of his career in 2006.

That world title didn't define his legacy. By that point, Mossy Oak Mudslinger had long since established himself as a legend among legends. Nevertheless, he was the sentimental favorite among bull riders in his sixth and final season.

"Knowing he was going to retire soon, they voted for him," said Lambert, who acknowledged that riders voted with their hearts that year. "I don't blame them, but we had to change the rules because of that."

It was because of that the PBR changed its way of determining how it awards the World Champion Bull. Now the riders' votes determine the Top 5 contenders who then compete during the World Finals with the highest total bull score earning the title.

"If you asked me if Mudslinger was the greatest bull of all time, I could argue either way in that conversation," Lambert said. "I feel so strongly that he's one of the best bulls there's ever been." ✪

Stock Contractors

Dillon Page took a chance. It was 1985, the Oklahoma peanut farmer had hit tough times, and the future looked bleak. On a hunch, he laid out a dollar a pound for a trailer full of bucking heifers.

Today, his bucking stock sales bring in around $1.5 million a year. Times aren't so tough anymore.

Page's story is similar to countless others', whose successes as breeders and stock contractors have paralleled that of the PBR.

To say any bull can buck is like saying any horse can win the Kentucky Derby—it's simply not true. Today, after years of selective breeding, meticulous registration, and no small amount of hit-and-miss, the American Bucking Bull has become its own breed.

But finding the best is no easy task. PBR Livestock Director Cody Lambert spends hours every week poring over video tapes and visiting ranches to scout the superstars.

Some breeders have had more success than others. The Pages (Dillon and his son, H.D.) have won the coveted Stock Contractor of the Year title six times. Chad Berger of North Dakota has won it twice.

And it's not limited to multi-generational ranching families. Tom Teague, a self-made truck-leasing mogul, has been instrumental in building the PBR and owns a number of superstar bulls, including Little Yellow Jacket and 2008 World Champion Bones. Celebrities like comedian Larry the Cable Guy and NFL quarterback Chad Pennington have also gotten into the game.

Like the PBR itself, the breeding business has moved from hot and dusty sale barns to become a multi-million dollar enterprise. ✪

Tom Teague (right) jokes with bull rider Matt Bohon (middle) and PBR CEO Randy Bernard. Teague has owned championship bulls for years, but the 2008 World Champion Bones was the first he personally raised from a calf.

Chad Berger has twice been voted Stock Contractor of the Year. It is an honor to be selected by the top 40 riders in the world.

The red ear tags and unmistakable brands along his flanks made Mudslinger an easy bull to identify and helped build his celebrity status. Toys, clothing, and even a coin-operated kiddie ride all bear his name.

Mossy Oak Mudslinger could drop even the best riders in the world. Shown here in his last out, the retiring star grounds eventual World Champion Guilherme Marchi.

"Red Wolf was the Jerry Rice of bucking bulls," said Ty Murray when the great bull passed away in 2006, at the geriatric age of 18. The celebrity bull was responsible for three of the top 15 highest scores of all time, including a 96-pointer with Bubba Dunn in 1999. "If he bucked a guy off in two or three seconds he would just take a victory lap," said Cody Lambert. "But if he was ridden for seven or eight seconds he was mad and was looking for somebody to run over. It didn't matter if it was a bull rider, bull fighter, or judge. At the 1997 PBR World Finals, he was ridden, and while one of the judges was calculating the score, Red Wolf ran him over. We had to bring in an alternate judge to finish the round."

Troubadour, named and raised by the late Mikel Moreno, has been a title contender for the past two years. Picked on by other bulls as a youngster, the banana-horned California bull has become perhaps the most popular among PBR riders, guaranteeing scores in the 90s—provided they can hang on.

Pampered and protected, the bulls of the PBR enjoy a lifestyle the typical bovine could never imagine. They are generally fed more than 40 pounds of grain and alfalfa a day, and never travel more than 8 hours at a time. The PBR also employs bucking chutes that are specially designed to prevent leg injuries.

Still living up to his name in the Las Vegas holding pens in 2008, World Champion Bull Bones was a gangly youngster when he won the title. He's since put on hundreds of pounds and remains a favorite of Tom Teague, his owner, who raised him from a calf.

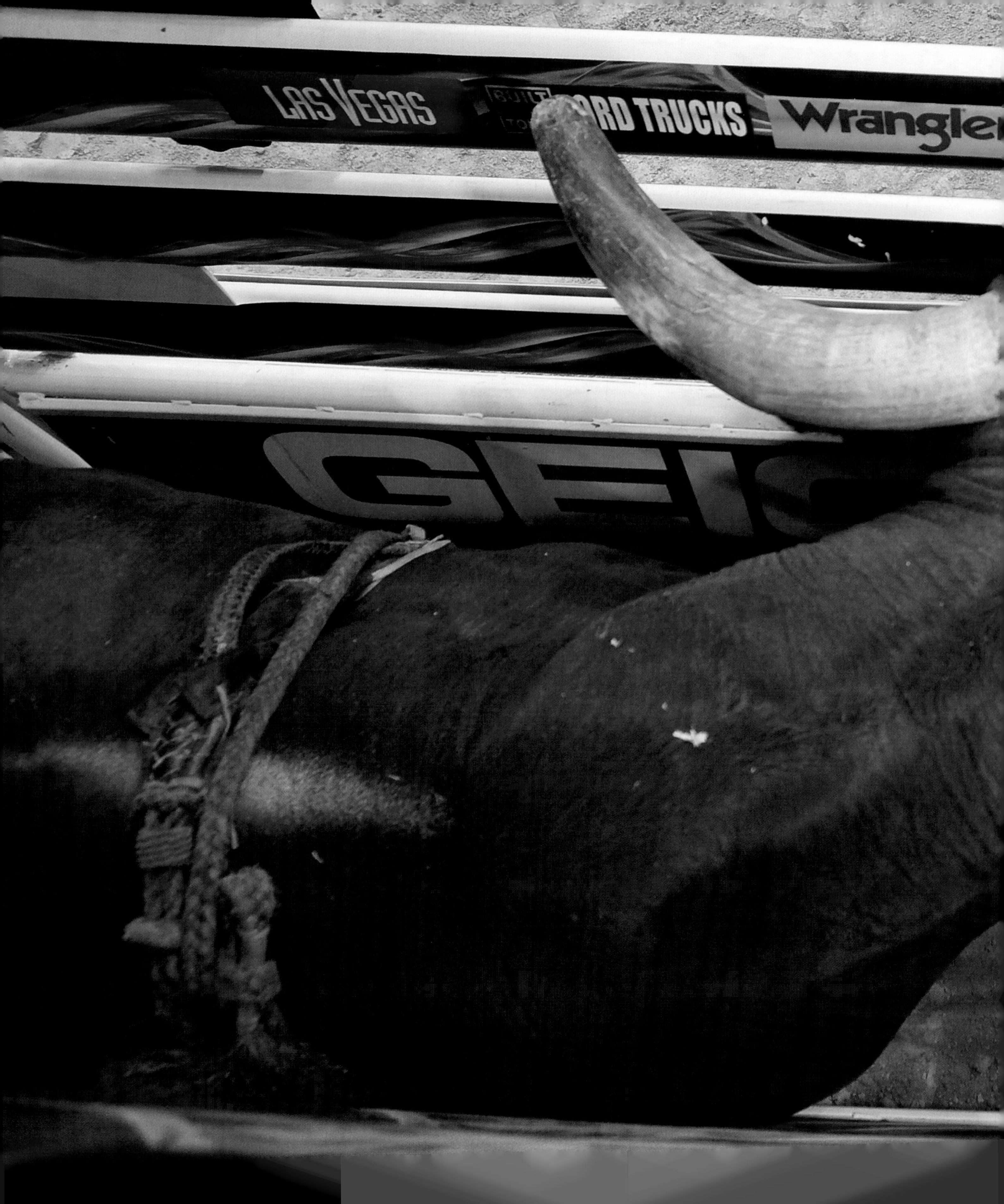
LAS VEGAS
BUILT
ORD TRUCKS
Wrangle
GEIC

The massive horns of California Dreamin' are sure to give even the bravest rider second thoughts as he climbs onto the animal's back. For many, the few seconds spent in the narrow chute are the most frightening of the night. As one rider put it: "Metal doesn't give. Bone does."

Tito Martinez's Gnash holds the distinction of having sidelined Justin McBride in 2007. Upon his return to competition, McBride had his revenge, scoring 93.75 points on him in July of the following year.

A huge animal, Chicken on a Chain tips the scales at close to a ton. The handsome bull, partially owned by comedian Larry the Cable Guy, was 2007 World Champion and rarely puts up ride scores lower than 90.

Snotty, messy, and perpetually scowling, Big Bucks was the 2005 World Champion Bull and a favorite on tour until his retirement in 2008. The black bucker would never have won Mr. Congeniality, however. His handler, Greg Simino, says "He's a little tight-wound, muscled-out dude, and he'll take on anyone if they bother him or try to socialize."

Chicken on a Chain rests contentedly in his North Carolina stall. "He's kind of a throwback to the old style of bucking bulls. He's quite a bit bigger than most of them these days, and he has all the qualities that a great one of any era has," says Cody Lambert of the black-and-white monster. "He's pretty catty for a bull that weighs 1,900 pounds."

Remarkably, many of the bulls at PBR events get along quite well. Many have been raised together since they were calves and are perfectly content to travel together.

Clowns no more. The protection bullfighters of the PBR, once known as rodeo clowns, traded in their makeup and baggy clothes for athletic uniforms in 2003. Insanely brave and tough, each one of them has endured a staggering amount of injuries during the course of their work.

The Lifesavers

✪

Chapter Four

The Bullfighters

The rider hits the dirt like a sack of wet concrete. The bull feels it, turns, and searches for the man—the small, two-legged thing who insulted his dignity.

The bull sees him. The man is hurt, slow to move. The bull charges. From nowhere, two human streaks flash by his wild eyes. They are Joe Baumgartner and Shorty Gorham, and this is their job. They've drawn the bull's attention. He turns to chase them, forgetting about the man on the ground. Frank Newsom comes in from another direction and the bull turns to him.

The rider is up. He limps to the gate. He survives.

The Dickies DuraBullfighters are the guardian angels of the PBR. They spend six to nine hours every weekend keeping the top 45 bull riders in the world alive. On a good day, they'll simply need to distract the bulls long enough for the rider to get to safety. But when a rider becomes entangled, they leap in to get his hands free. They've been known to shield downed riders with their own bodies.

"I think the bullfighters save my butt more than I even realize," says PBR rider Kody Lostroh.

"Bull riding would end pretty quickly without them," adds Wiley Petersen.

The bullfighter's uniform has changed over the years. The oversized clothing which once lent itself to the "rodeo clown" image has evolved into a loose-fitting jersey and shorts, allowing for maximum mobility. The size of the garments serves another purpose: it makes the bullfighter a bigger target. In the words of Frank Newsom, "The bull might think he's got you when he's just got your shorts."

The bullfighter's vest is notably different from those worn by the cowboys. Though both vests feature break-away construction in the event a rider or fighter is hooked, the bullfighter's is worn underneath his other garments, and features hard plastic outer shells on the front and back, unlike the riders'. ✪

In between outs, there's always a little time for fooling around. Shorty Gorham, Frank Newsom, and Shane "Mad Dog" Simpson get their groove on at the 2008 PBR World Finals.

Shorty Gorham provides some distraction as Ross Coleman (left) slips away unharmed. The goal of the bullfighter is to take the animal's attention off the rider. Once accomplished, the next step is to stay alive. Surprisingly, this usually involves standing still while the animal charges, then making a quick movement to the side. Trying to outrun a bull is neither practical nor possible.

Shorty Gorham rushes in to save Renato Nunes at the 2007 PBR World Finals. When a rider comes off the bull the wrong way, even the best bullfighters can't always prevent catastrophe. "Some guys have a tendency of always getting off the bull badly," Gorham says. "Then there are others who time their bounces and land on their feet. We don't have to do much for them."

Shorty Gorham jukes left, while Joe Baumgartner prepares to come in from the other side. The chemistry between bullfighters is vital. They must work together instinctively, with split-second timing.

se Byrne, a newcomer to the Built Ford Tough
ies, stepped in when veteran Joe Baumgartner
s hurt at the 2008 World Finals. The youngster's
mplete lack of hesitation earned him immediate
pect.

move in to keep the animal *while another will attempt to pull the tail of the rope off over the rider's fingers.*

Joe Baumgartner leaps onto a bull's back to free a rider's hung-up hand. Shane "Mad Dog" Simpson does his best to slow the animal, while Frank Newsom prepares for another shot at the tangled rope. "There is no formula," Newsom says. "You just react."

NAMPA
INVITATIONAL
PBR
NAMPA
INVITATIONAL
Wrangler
Wrangler
BUILT
Ford
TOUGH
Wrangler

As this photo shows, bulls will most often try to butt or spear a rider rather than trample him. But there are exceptions to every rule. The barrel in the background has been a standard piece of safety equipment for decades. It offers an island of protection for an athlete who finds himself beyond reach of the fence.

Getting one's hand free from the rope during a buckoff is crucial. Here, Leonil Santos finds himself flying right while his hand remains firmly in the rope.

After freeing a rider, Shorty Gorham gets launched in Albuquerque in 2008. The impact on his return trip would fracture a vertebra, keeping him out of action for two months.

DANIEL'S®

JACK DANIEL'S REMIND YOU TO DRINK RESPONSIBLY

Former schoolteacher and all-around athlete Flint Rasmussen has become as integral to the PBR's live events as the bull riders themselves. "All I ever wanted was to be an entertainer, and this sport is my avenue to do that," he once said. "I'm like a kid who always gets to be the center of attention all the time. I love it."

Flint Rasmussen

The PBR might not be the first place you'd expect to see black socks with shorts. But if you do, you're probably looking at Flint Rasmussen.

Rasmussen is the PBR's live entertainer. Sometimes called "the barrel man"—a throwback to the days when rodeo clowns cracked wise when they weren't getting speared while in a padded barrel by enthusiastic bovines—Rasmussen fills the gaps in competition created by television commercial breaks with singing, dancing, and general tomfoolery.

Entirely through his own talents, Rasmussen has become as important to the live shows as the bull riders themselves. He's so popular, in fact, that the perennial "Cowboy Hunks of the PBR" calendar doubled its sales when he made his pictorial debut.

The former schoolteacher started honing his comedic chops early on. "As a kid, I would dream about entertaining people," he says. "I'd take a tennis racket and turn on some music and play it like a guitar."

Rasmussen won accolades as a three-time National Circuit Finals barrel man, four-time Canadian National Finals Rodeo barrel man, eight-time Wrangler National Finals Rodeo barrel man, and eight-time winner of the PRCA Rodeo Clown of the Year. Despite his great physical condition—he is easily the fittest athlete on tour—the 40-year-old suffered a heart attack in March 2009. Just six weeks later, he was back in action. It seems you can't keep a good man down.

Rasmussen lives in Choteau, Montana, with his wife Katie and two daughters, Shelby Rae and Paige. When his touring schedule allows, he raises performance horses. ✪

Years ago, "rodeo clowns" served a dual purpose: they protected cowboys from the bulls and entertained the crowd with on-dirt antics. Eventually, the comic stylings became the responsibility of a single clown, called the barrel man, who spent most of his time in and around the safety barrel in the arena. Rasmussen represents the final evolution of that separation of duties. While he's still occasionally called a barrel man, his role is strictly entertainment.

Rasmussen doesn't need the makeup, but he wears it as a sign of respect for the traditions of rodeo clowns. The son and brother of rodeo announcers, he has great affection for the lifestyle. He worked his way through college with his act.

Rasmussen insists that his in-arena persona is strictly a character. But no one who has ever met him can deny his gregariousness and approachability.

The painted smile is almost unnecessary; Rasmussen's positive attitude and passion for bull riding is infectious.

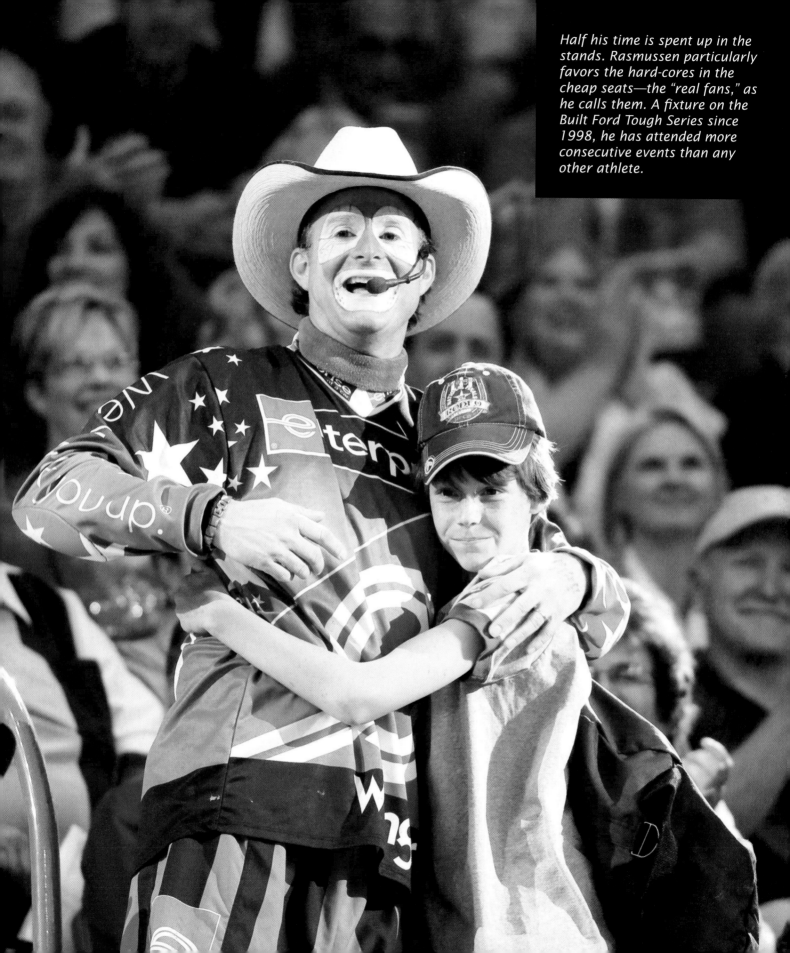

Half his time is spent up in the stands. Rasmussen particularly favors the hard-cores in the cheap seats—the "real fans," as he calls them. A fixture on the Built Ford Tough Series since 1998, he has attended more consecutive events than any other athlete.

Rasmussen's 2009 heart attack caught the entire Western world by surprise. Even at age 40, he was widely considered the healthiest person in the PBR. An exercise fanatic, he's been frustrated trying to get back to his old form, though few would say he looks any less fit.

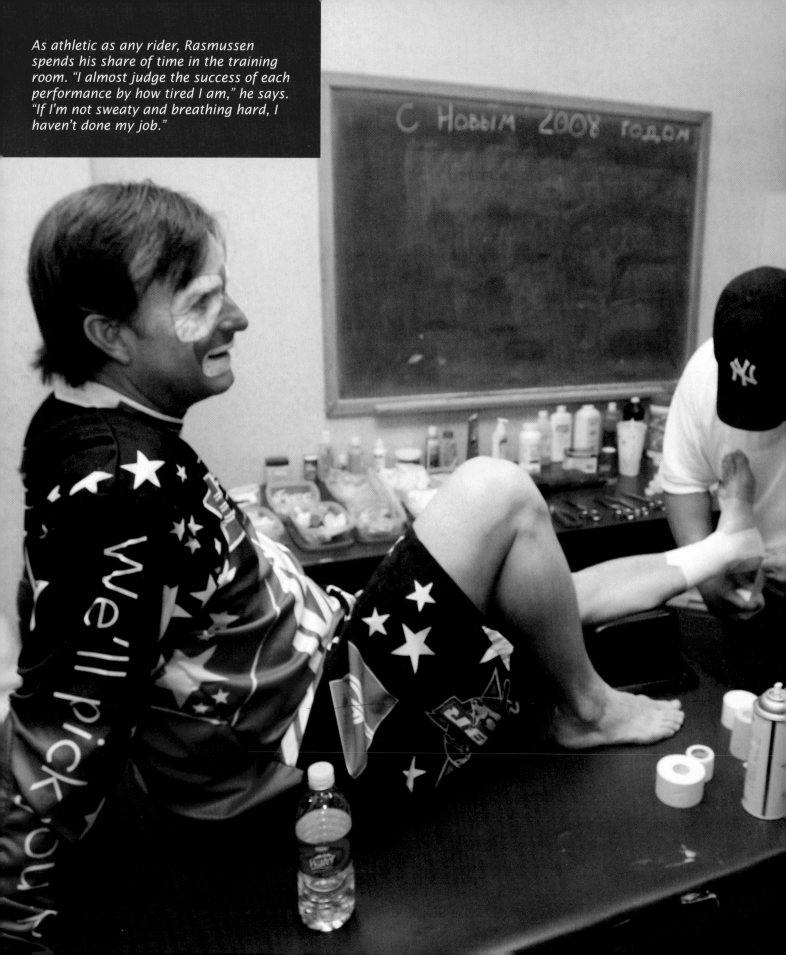

As athletic as any rider, Rasmussen spends his share of time in the training room. "I almost judge the success of each performance by how tired I am," he says. "If I'm not sweaty and breathing hard, I haven't done my job."

There's a quiet side to the barrel man. Though he would easily be feted by any of his thousands of fans in cities across the country, Rasmussen usually heads straight back to the hotel after a performance to unwind and conserve his energy for the next performance.

The Medical Team

"Every time these guys go out there to ride," says Dr. Tandy Freeman, "there is a realistic risk of being maimed or killed."

Freeman, a Texas-based orthopedic surgeon, has been the director of medical services for the PBR for years. The soft-spoken medic has witnessed the kinds of injuries usually seen in war zones. He and his staff are on hand for every Built Ford Tough Series event, along with two ambulance crews.

Freeman says that the most common injury in bull riding is a concussion. He is currently conducting a multi-year study to determine the long-term effects of concussions on professional bull riders.

There is an art to doctoring riders. These are men whose livelihood depends on riding, people for whom a few aspirin and a six-pack of beer are typical remedies.

"There's a difference between hurting and being hurt," says Freeman. "Hurting is when you're sore and have the usual lumps, bumps, and bruises. Being hurt is when it adversely affects a rider's ability to compete. My job is to help these guys figure out the difference." ✪

Doctor Tandy Freeman, the unflappable head of PBR sports medicine, is the most sought-after physician in the Western sports world. A Dallas-based orthopedist, he has the unenviable position of telling headstrong young men whether or not they're ready to ride.

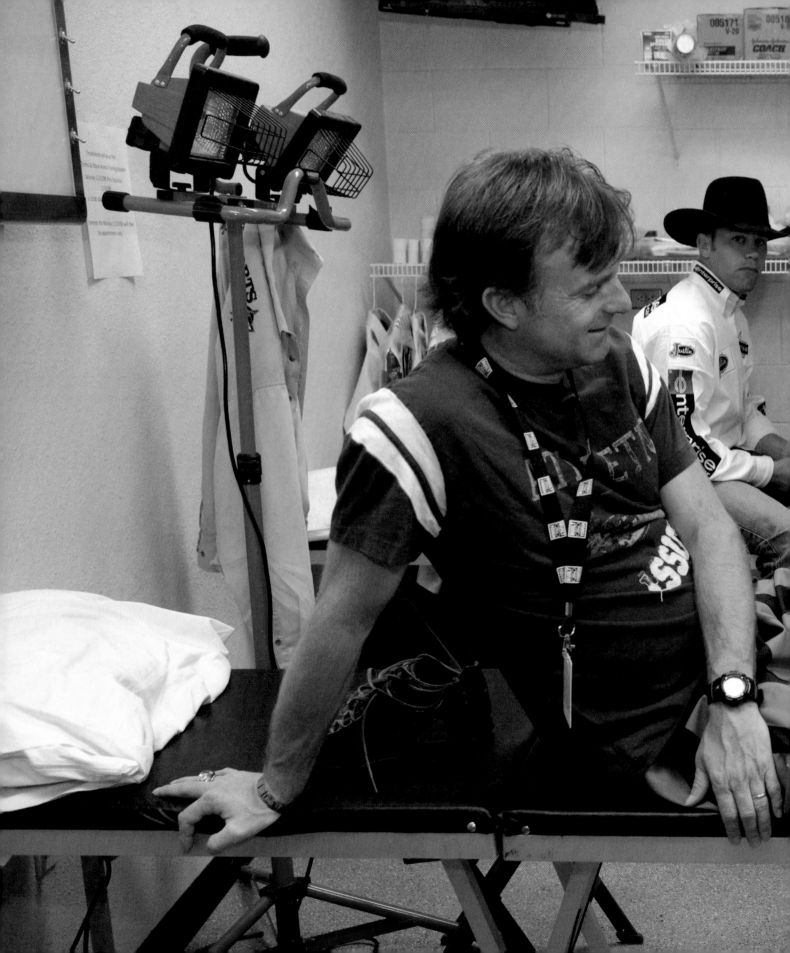

Tape, tape, and more tape. In the PBR, if you don't ride, you don't get paid. As a result, the training room is almost always filled with athletes looking for temporary fixes to nagging injuries.

The Legends

Mike White (left) and Chris Shivers (right) are close friends—and two of the legendary athletes of bull riding. White is a PRCA World Champion and PBR Rookie of the Year, and Shivers is a two-time PBR World Champion.

⭐

Chapter Five

Every generation has its own heroes. But legends live forever.

They are men whose accomplishments transcend mere numbers and statistics, who are on a level all their own.

No three men define the modern era of professional bull riding more than Justin McBride, Chris Shivers, and Adriano Moraes. Together, the trio has won a combined seven world titles in the first 15 years of the PBR. More importantly, the three men stand as a validation of the determination of the PBR's 20 founding fathers. They represent the unified dream of those who came before them.

Along with their gold buckles and millions of dollars in earnings, McBride, Shivers, and Moraes continue to serve the sport they love as its ambassadors. ⭐

Perhaps the single-most naturally talented bull rider in history, Justin McBride shocked the world when he announced his retirement at the end of the 2008 season.

Justin McBride

"I just don't like doing it anymore, so I'm quitting."

That was the sobering sentiment from Justin McBride, who, on October 21, 2008, formally announced his retirement from the PBR at an afternoon press conference in Las Vegas.

"It's something I put a lot of thought into," said the two-time World Champion during his opening remarks. "I'm pretty excited about the decision. I feel like I've done everything I set out to do in this sport."

It was only fitting that McBride would choose to make his statement in the city where his career became the stuff legends are made of. One of the most decorated bull riders in PBR history, the two-time World Champion was the first bull rider to ever win more than $5 million in career earnings, making him the richest cowboy in history.

In his 10-year career, McBride set an extensive list of records, including 32 career event wins, the most money earned in a single season ($1,835,321), and eight single-season event wins, among many others.

"Sometimes people get to thinking you're retiring from life," said McBride, who in his first year of eligibility was inducted into the PBR Ring of Honor. "I'm just retiring from the sport that I've done for most of my life.

"I have done what I wanted to do: win a PBR world title," he said. "Now I am in a position to go out while I'm healthy and still riding well. I mean, you can get hurt crossing the street, but there are more risks involved with bull riding.

"Now that I have a family and a child to think about, I want to be able to retire and enjoy my life with them and not be a crippled bull rider."

Since he retired, he's spent the majority of his time at his ranch near Elk City, Oklahoma, while also pursuing a music career. He plans to continue his broadcasting career with Versus and other sponsor-related activities.

Bull riding is the "only thing I've ever done to this point," he remarked, but his short-term plans included a lot of hunting and fishing.

On the ramp of the Thomas & Mack Center, McBride walked to his second world title in 2007. "It's really fun to show up, and the only thing you're thinking about is winning the event," he said. "That's a really good feeling to have."

McBride was good...almost too good. Controversy erupted at times when judges gave him high marks for what looked like easy rides. Trouble was, they weren't easy. He just made them look that way.

McBride is not a big man—at 5'9", he's about average for a bull rider—but what he lacked in size he more than made up for in grit. The Elk City, Oklahoma, cowboy rode with broken ribs, punctured lungs, and smashed ankles.

McBride was one of those rare cowboys whose ability, looks, and charisma put him in the same category as legends like Jim Shoulders, Larry Mahan, and Ty Murray. Today he brings his experience and insight into the broadcasting booth.

Shortly after his 2007
championship win, McBride
(shown here with Brendon Clark
and Ross Coleman) surpassed
$5 million in career earnings—a
record in the Western riding
world. Only 10 years before, he
was crushing rock in a gravel pit.

A PBR announcer once described McBride in three words: "Cowboy, cowboy, cowboy."

In the 140-year history of Western riding sports, no one was as naturally talented as McBride. He could make the ugliest ride something to remember.

Quick to smile and completely comfortable in his own skin, McBride was one of the most popular riders on tour. Most nights after events, he could be found at the hotel bar strumming a guitar and singing cowboy songs.

Camo twice propelled McBride to greatness. The brindle mulie was the decisive ride in both his 2005 and 2007 title campaigns. The first ride was unforgettably forgettable: McBride needed only to cover to win the championship, and ended up on the side of the bull for an ugly 72-pointer. But it was enough to win.

Once claiming that his idea of physical therapy was "sitting on the couch drinking beer," McBride could go for weeks or months without even thinking about bull riding, then come back and win almost immediately. He missed the first half of 2008 because of shoulder surgery. He returned in June and won Tulsa two weeks later.

The bull riding world lost a star when McBride retired, but the music world may have gained one. McBride is rolling the dice with a career in country music, and it seems to be working. Within a year of leaving the sport, McBride sang on the stage of the Grand Ole Opry.

Chris Shivers

The Cajun cowboy knows all too well what can happen in eight seconds. Shivers has won two world championships, but in the five-plus years since his last title, he's broken numerous bones—his ankle, fibula, and tibia at the Hawaii All Star Challenge in November 2006—and his left eye socket in a chute mishap in April 2008. But it wasn't until he broke his nose in Baltimore that the hard-nosed cowboy knew it was time to do things differently.

"It's to a point now where I'm getting hit in the face," Shivers said, "I'm either going to wear the helmet or I'm going to stay home, so..." His voice trailed off and the 30-year-old, who is completing his 12th season on the Built Ford Tough Series, hesitated for a moment before he continued. "I don't really want to say that," he said, "but I'm not going to be one of those guys who is going to show up with a broken arm or fractured something and try to ride through all that stuff. I've been though all that and I've done that and it's not any fun when you show up hurt.... That's the difference between now and then."

Come to think of it, there are a few more differences. He was the first PBR millionaire, reaching the milestone when he was just 21, and then in January 2006 he became the first cowboy to earn $3 million. To date, he's second among all-time money earners with over $3.6 million in prize money.

Shivers is one of only three bull riders, along with Justin McBride and Adriano Moraes, who have won more than one world championship. He won the gold buckle in 2000 and then again in 2003. He also won the Challenger Tour title honors in 1997 and 2000.

The titles and earnings are impressive, but if there is one thing that defines Shivers, it's been his ability to make big rides in big moments.

He has made more 90-point rides—80 and counting—than anyone else in the PBR record books, and three of those rides are among the top 10 highest marked rides, including the highest-marked ride in PBR history of 96.5 points, a score he's accomplished twice. No one uses his feet better than Shivers.

Whether you analyze the Shivers of old or the helmet-wearing veteran of today, he is a virtual lock to one day be inducted into the PBR Ring of Honor.

When he's at th
game, no one
on the back of
Chris Shivers.
a battle-worn
the Built Ford
and his list of
is extraordina
addition to wir
World Champi
he's a two-tim
of the Challeng
and two-time
Lane Frost/Bre
Award for the
scored ride at
Finals.

Shivers and his best friend Mike White are nearly inseparable. For years, they were most easily disntinguished by their choice of hats—Shivers with his signature white hat, White with black. Among other endeavors, the pair now host their own bull riding school each summer.

Comparatively small, there's something about Shivers' body control that makes his rides a treat to watch. He is able to fully extend his legs and free arm without sacrificing balance, and can turn an 88-point bull into a 92.

By 2009, Shivers had racked up almost 80 90-point rides. No active rider is anywhere close to breaking that record. Ross Coleman, the closest competition, has just over 40.

Shivers has earned six of the highest 50 scores of all time. Among other things, he's twice tied the record for the highest score in history—96.5 points. He was also the first cowboy to reach the $1 million, $2 million, and $3 million marks.

Adriano Moraes: husband, father, mentor, trailblazer, ambassador, bull rider, legend.

Adriano Moraes

To fully understand Adriano Moraes the bull rider, one must first come to know Moraes the man. When Moraes first arrived in the U.S. at age 22, he left behind the tomato fields he'd been working in since his ninth birthday. He and his bride Flavia (they married just three months after meeting) arrived with only a few dollars, his riding skills, and little else.

Now, 17 years later, his name is permanently etched in the PBR's history books as its first World Champion (1994), first two-time World Champion (2001), and first three-time World Champion (2006). While his courage to excel has provided generations of young Brazilians with inspiration, his passion for bull riding and his love of life have made him a role model for everyone.

In his 15-year career, he competed in 229 Built Ford Tough Series events and claimed 29 event titles to go along with his unprecedented three world titles and more than $3 million in career earnings.

Over the course of his career, Moraes successfully rode 54 percent of his bulls with an average qualified score of 86.12 points. His forty-six 90-point rides, including a career-high 95 on Promiseland in Houston during the 2000 season, rank him as the third-highest behind only Justin McBride and Chris Shivers.

A perennial top-10 finisher in the world standings, only once did he finish outside of the top 20. The 14 times he has qualified for the PBR World Finals are more than any other rider since the event's inception.

It's been said that Moraes rides his best when the spotlight shines the brightest. Twice (in 1996 and again in 2006) he's been presented with the Lane Frost/Brent Thurman Award for the highest-marked ride at the World Finals.

It stands to reason that in 2009 Moraes joined McBride and J.W. Hart as the latest inductees into the prestigious PBR Ring of Honor.

In his own words, Moraes summed up his life when he wrote in his autobiography, "The man who carries my true identity is that tractor driver who built fences. Eight seconds are not enough to tell the story of a life of poverty, struggle, and love."

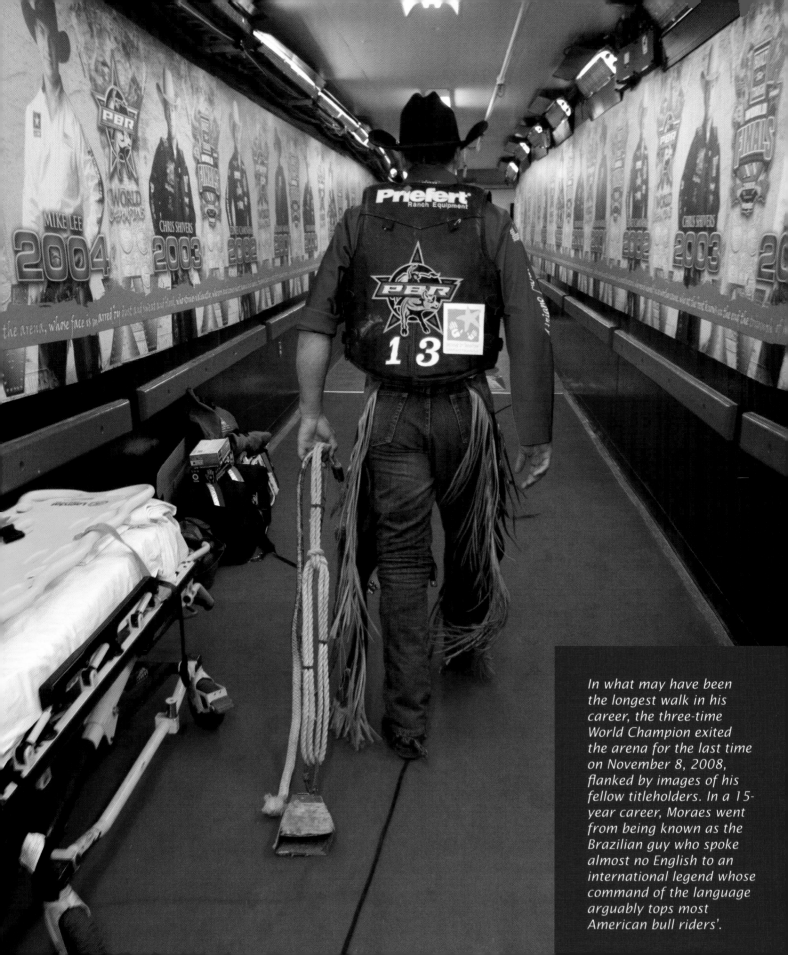

In what may have been the longest walk in his career, the three-time World Champion exited the arena for the last time on November 8, 2008, flanked by images of his fellow titleholders. In a 15-year career, Moraes went from being known as the Brazilian guy who spoke almost no English to an international legend whose command of the language arguably tops most American bull riders'.

Moraes prepares for his final ride. "I am going to be the first World Champion forever," he once said. "One hundred years from now, the third or fourth PBR World Champions won't be known, but they will always know the very first World Champion."

For years, Moraes was the oldest rider on tour and served as a surrogate father for many of the younger riders. Here, he counsels the 19-year-old Brian Canter—20 years his junior—after an injury in Tacoma, Washington, in 2007. "I try to be a good role model," he said. "Everyone has influence somehow, so everyone is responsible for everyone else. They deserve the best of me."

A devoted father, Moraes never missed an opportunity to coach his four sons. "Never quit," he told them after winning his third title against heavy odds.

Moraes, like most Brazilian athletes, is devoutly Catholic. Each year he flew a priest into Sin City to say mass each morning during the World Finals.

Blessed with boundless enthusiasm, Moraes was not above clowning around to break the tension behind the chutes.

The only man in PBR history to claim three World Championships, Moraes' efforts over eight rounds earned him $1.35 million. Broken down into eight eight-second blocks, that's an hourly wage of over $607 million.

Unwilling and unable to fully leave the sport he loves, Moraes snuck back into the arena after the final ride of his career to watch the remainder of the event from the obscurity of the shark cage. The champ remains fond of the press, but was willing to forego publicity in deference to the younger riders who had inherited his legacy.

Picture-perfect form and brute strength defined the riding style of Brazil's bridge builder.

Moraes' 2006 title came down to the final ride on the final day. Overcoming back spasms that would have hobbled a rhino, Moraes barely edged fellow countryman Guilherme Marchi.

An officially-retired Adriano Moraes bids farewell to 16,000 standing fans on November 8, 2008. "Life is a struggle," he said. "You win some, but most of the time you lose. If you have faith in God and faith in yourself, if you work hard, and your friends and family support you, you can do almost anything."

With the 2006 title secured, the three-time champ leapt into the stands to plant a dusty kiss on his wife, Flavia. She had come with him on his first trip to the U.S. in 1992 and she was with him the day he retired in 2008.